Cute Christmas

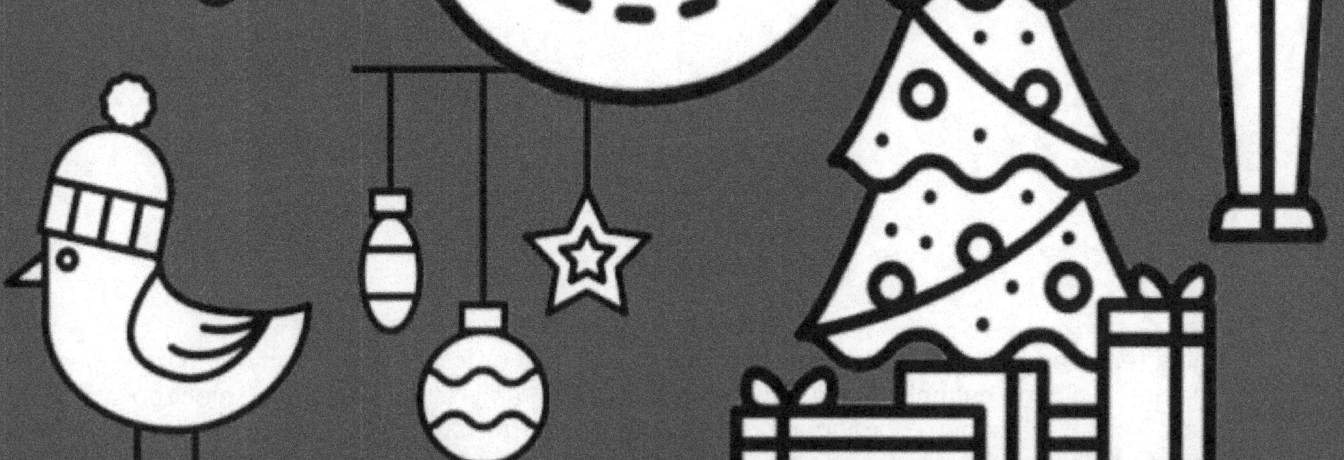

COLORING PAGES FOR KIDS AND ADULTS

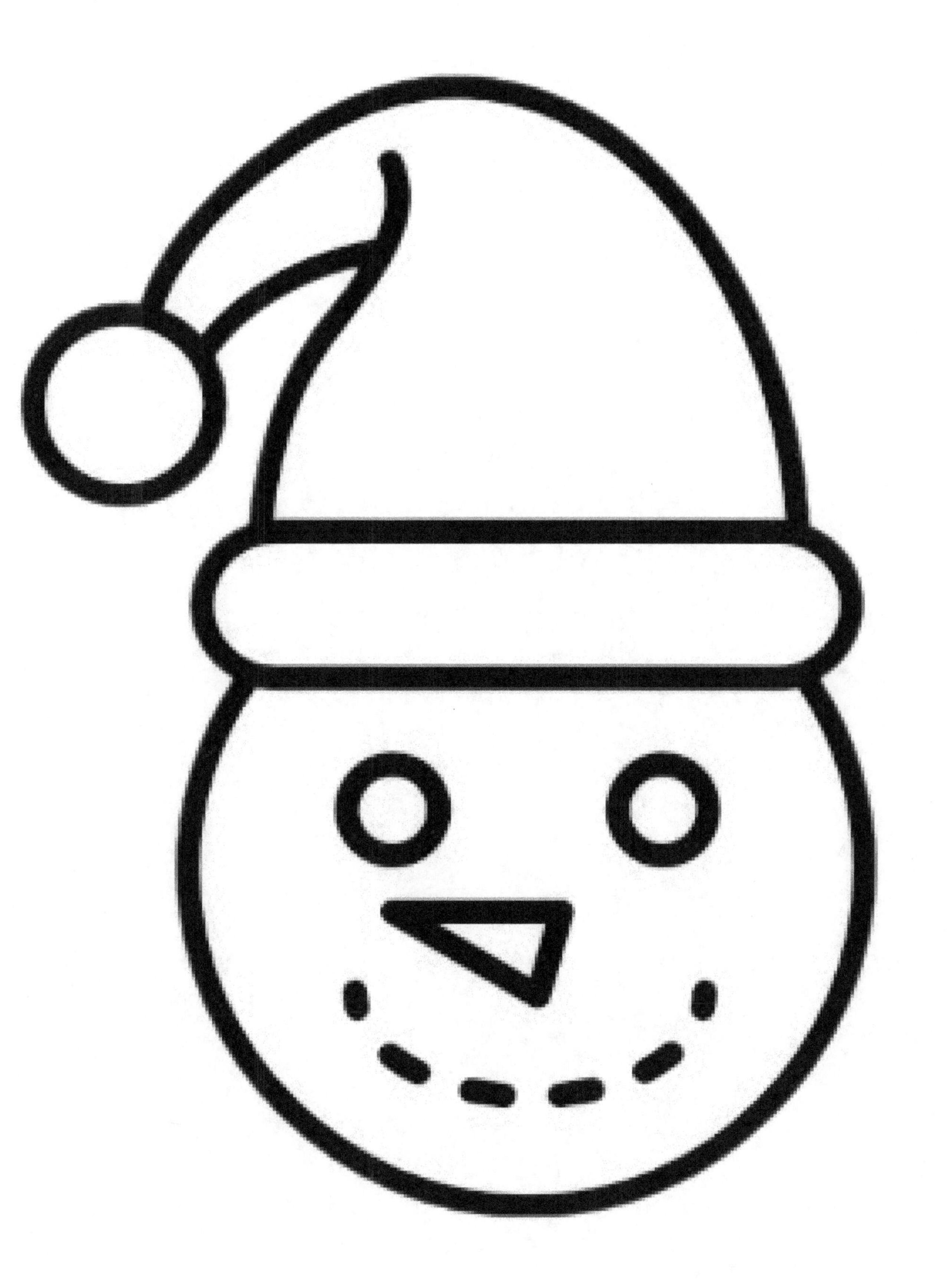

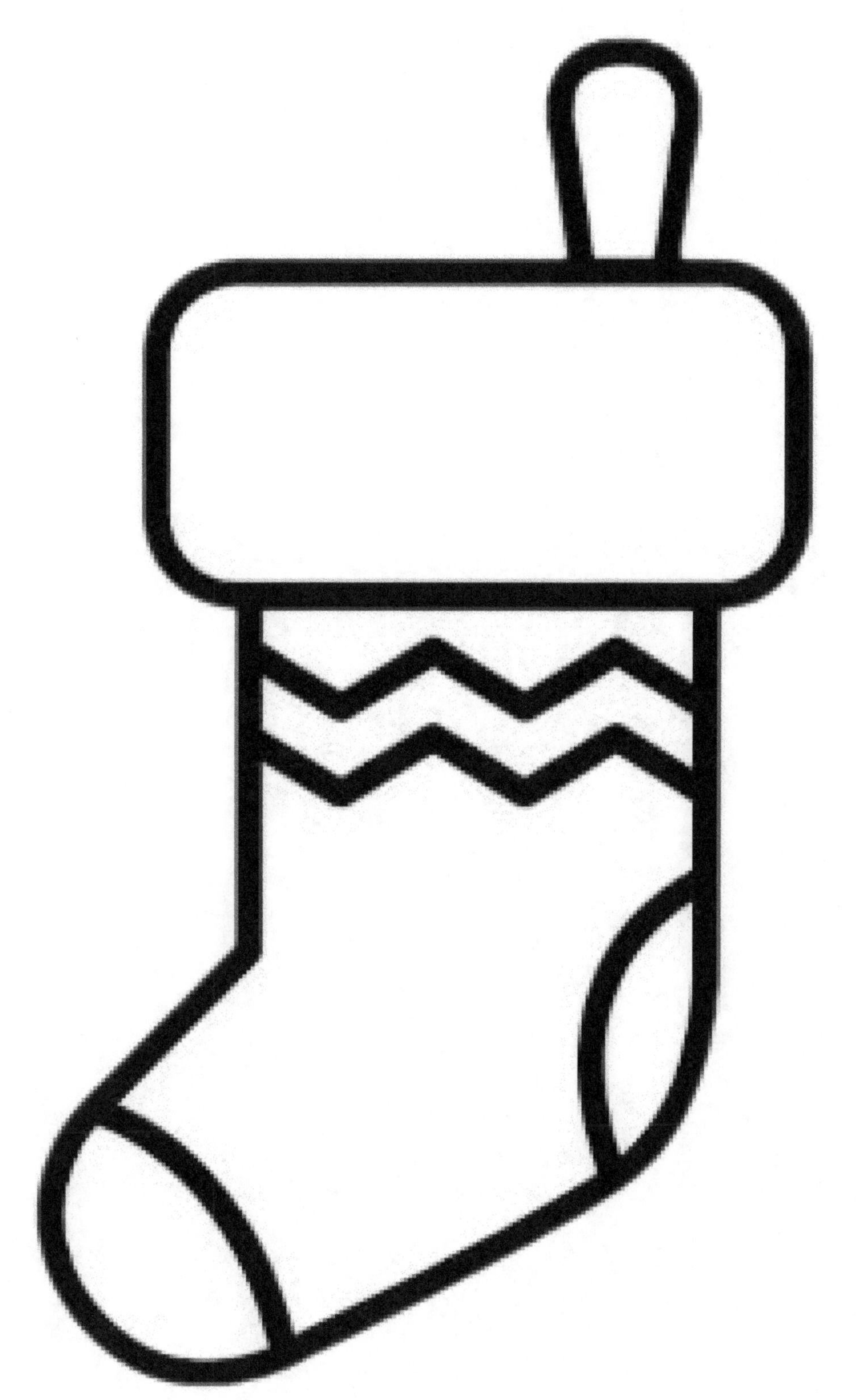

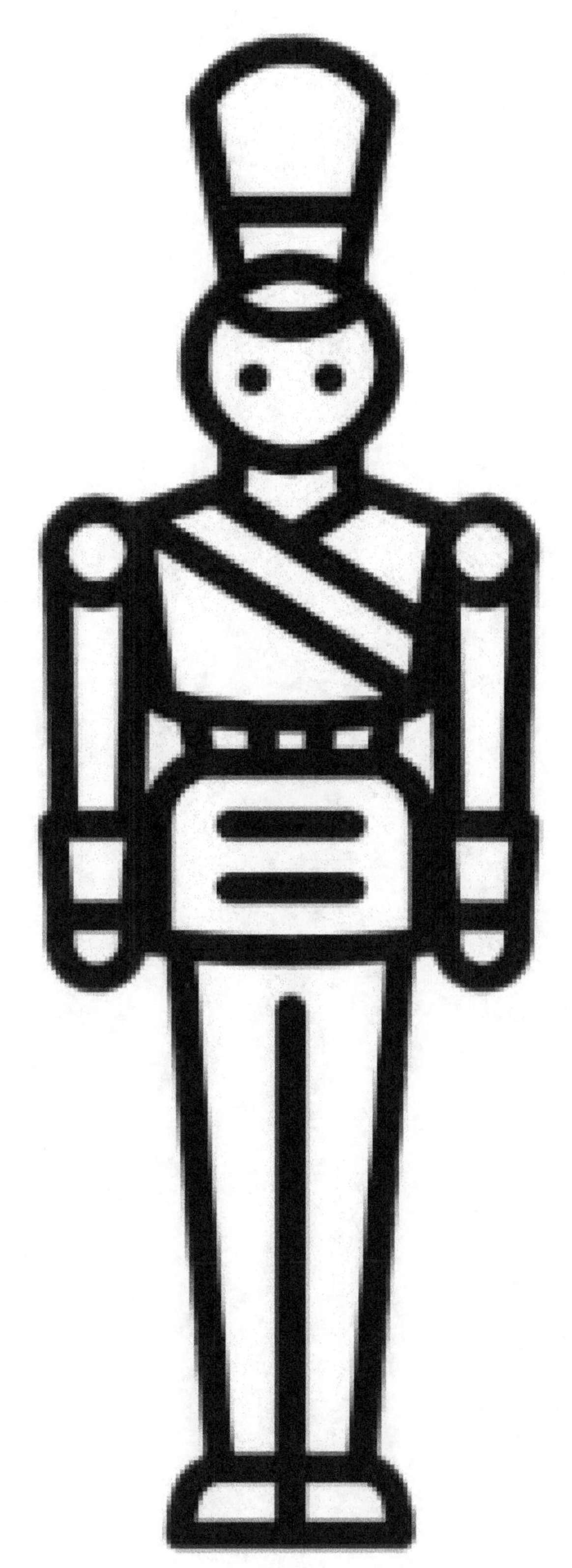

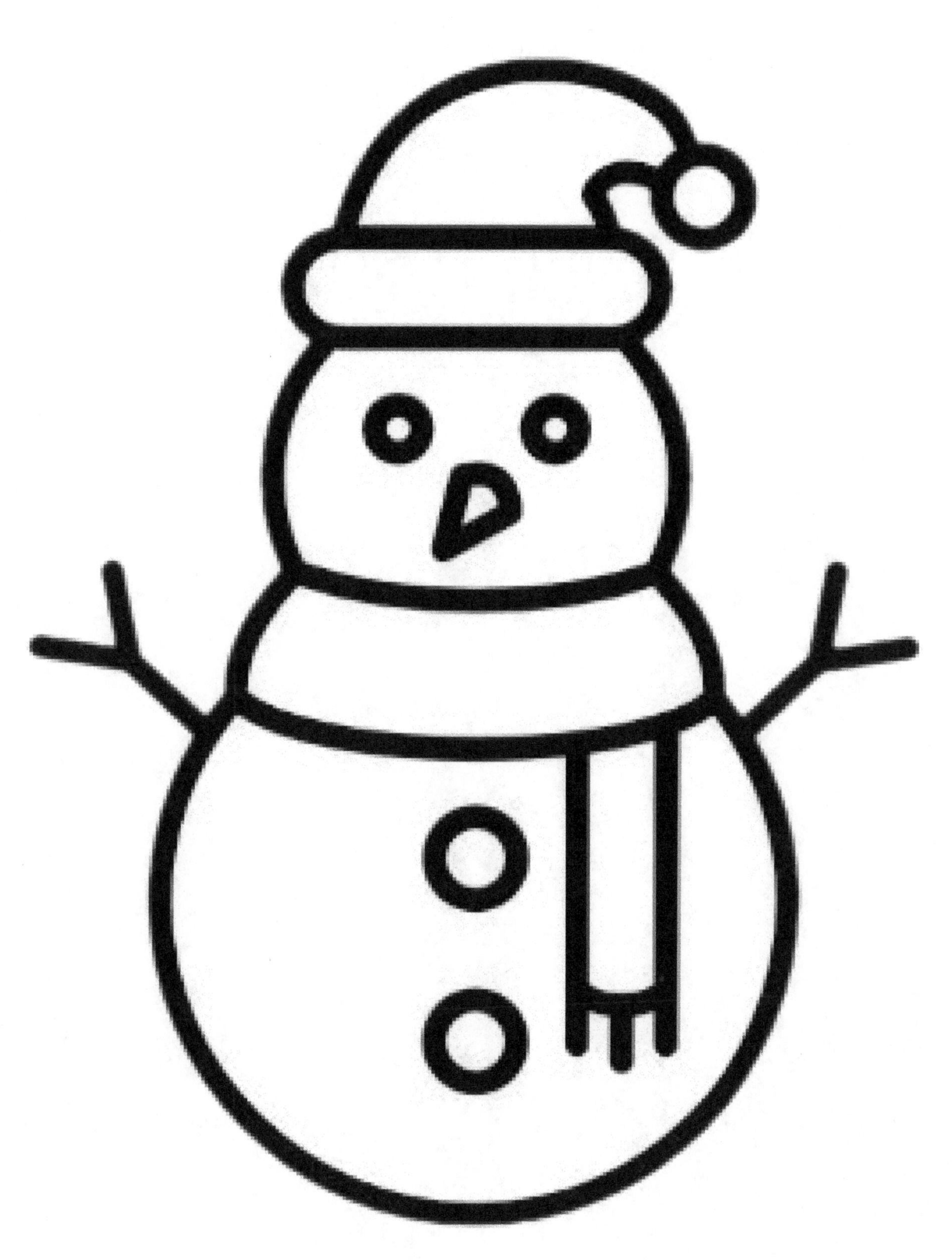

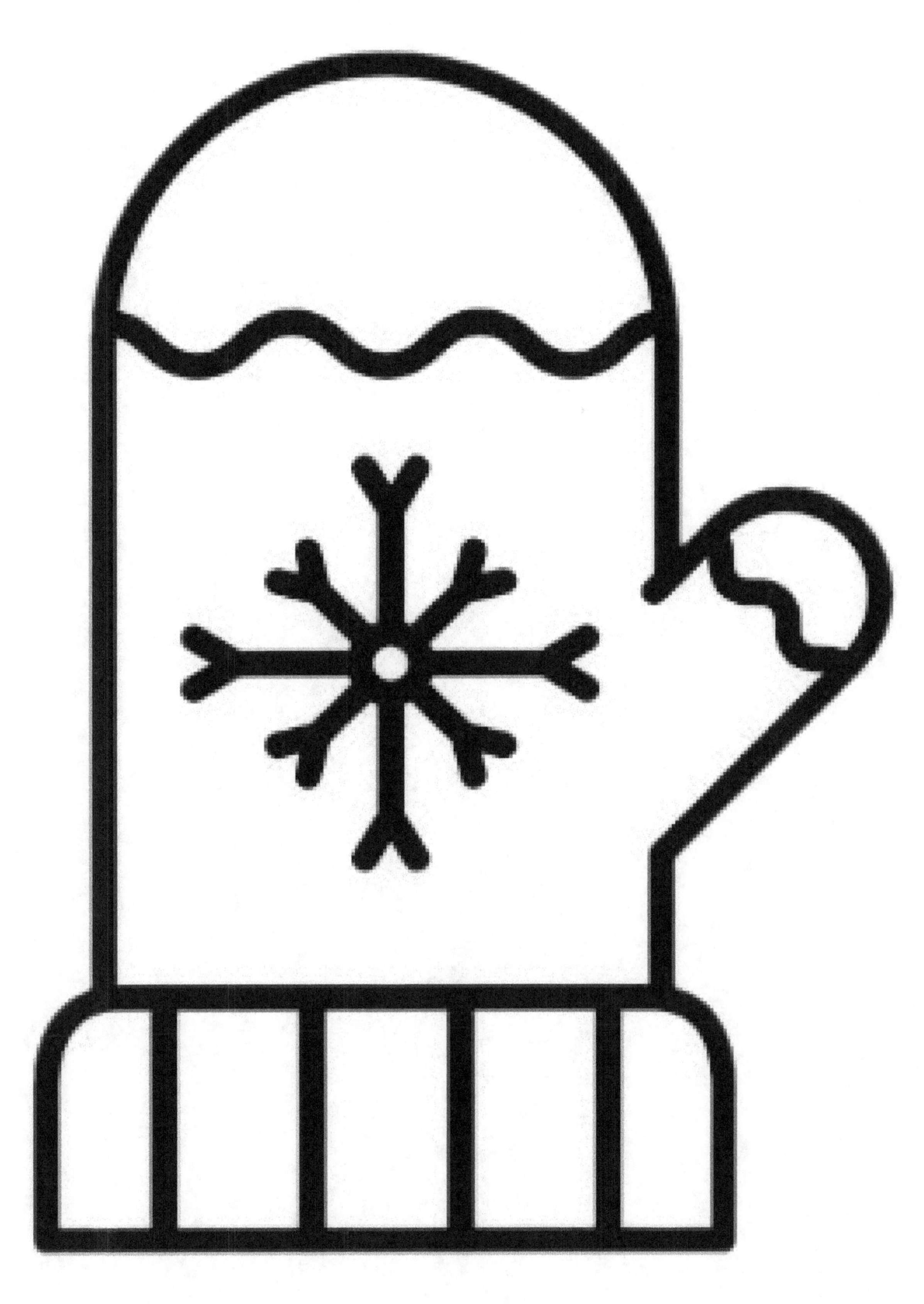

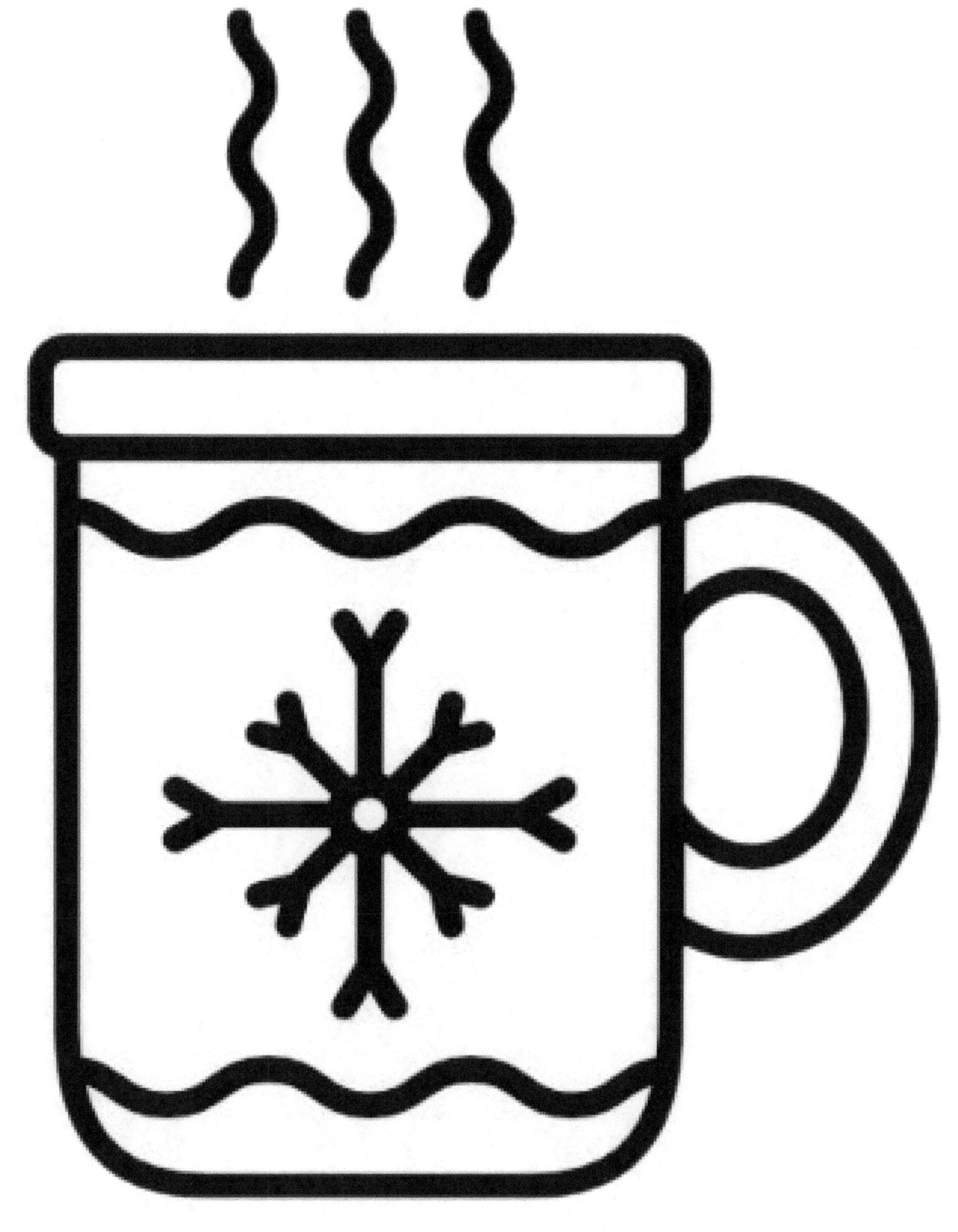

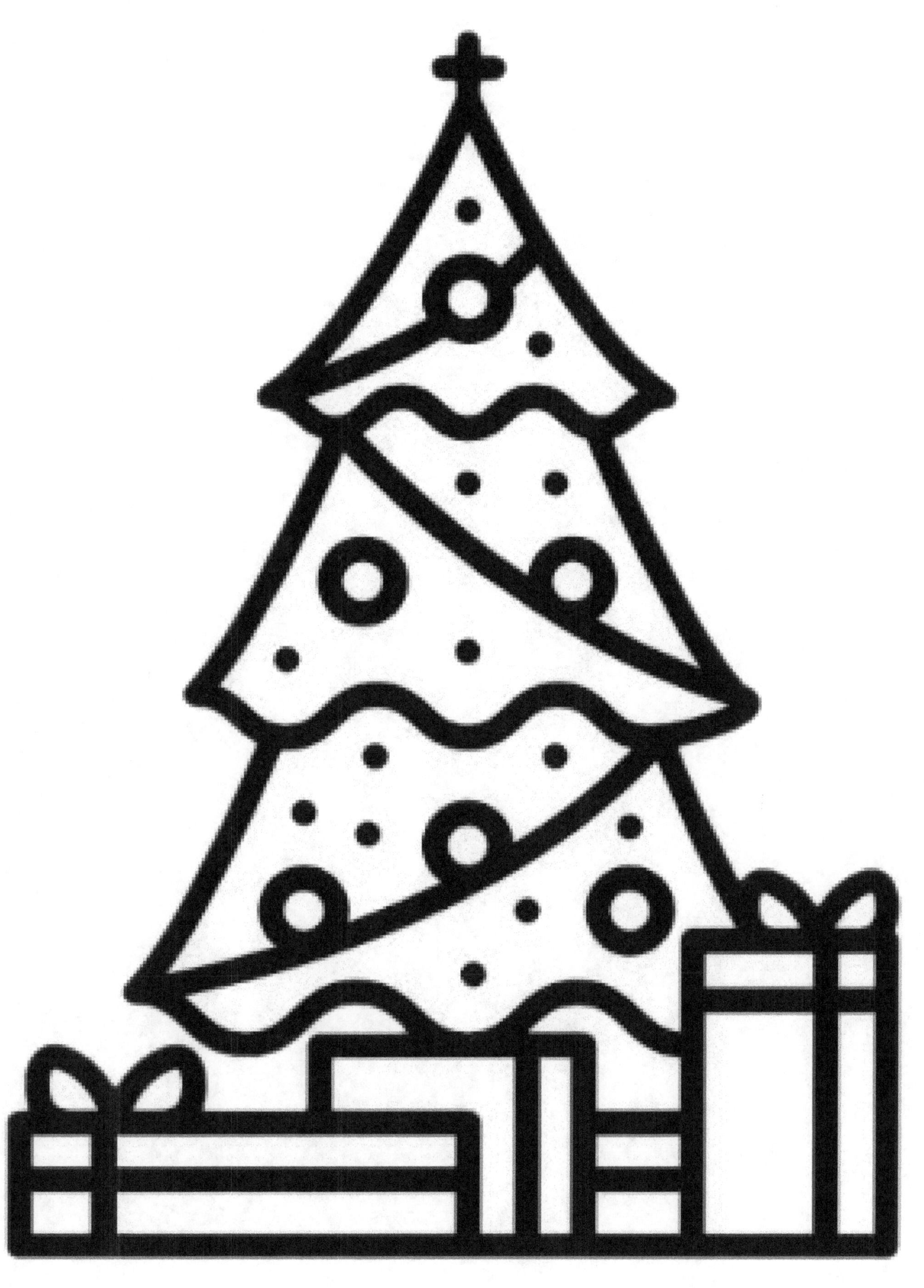

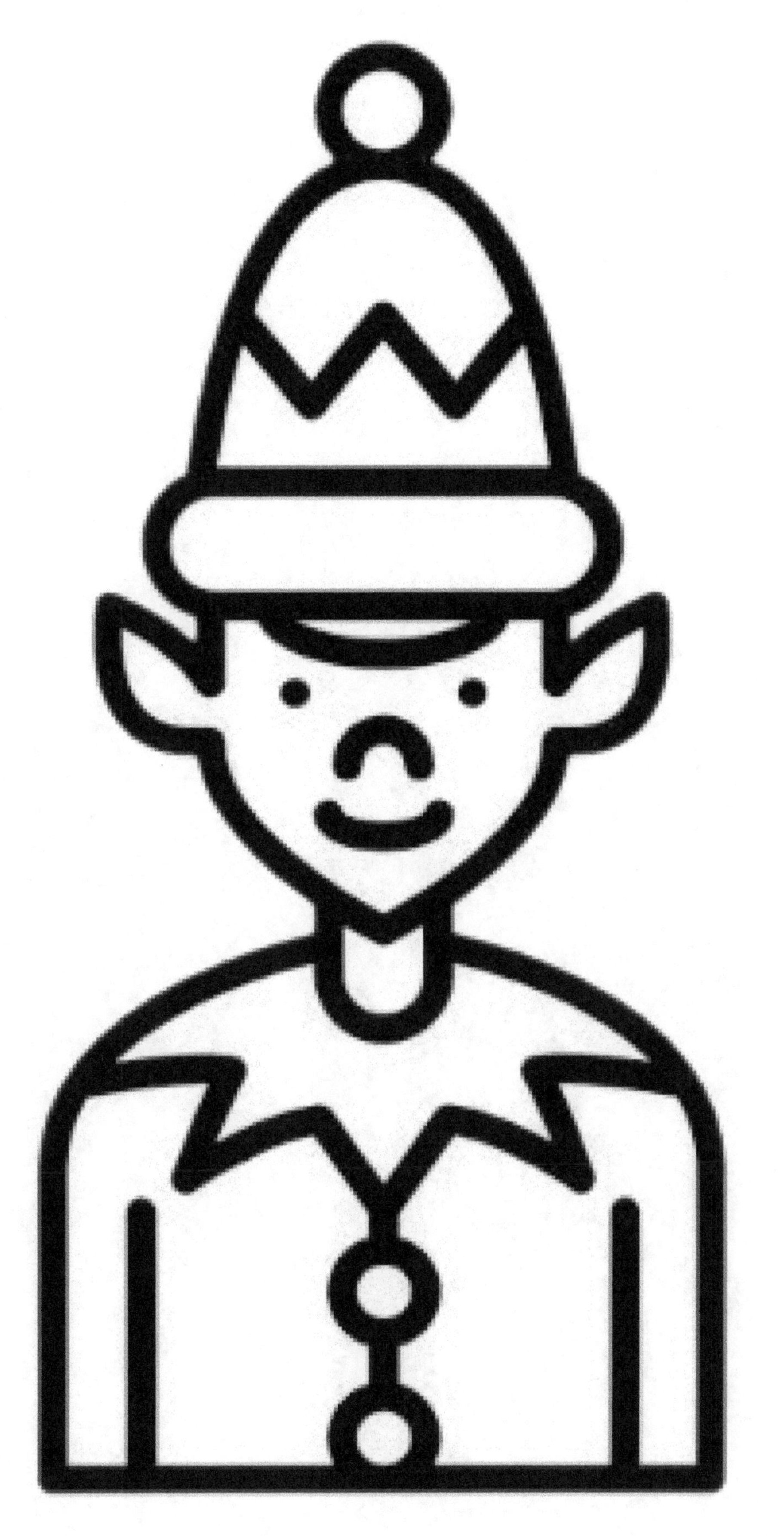

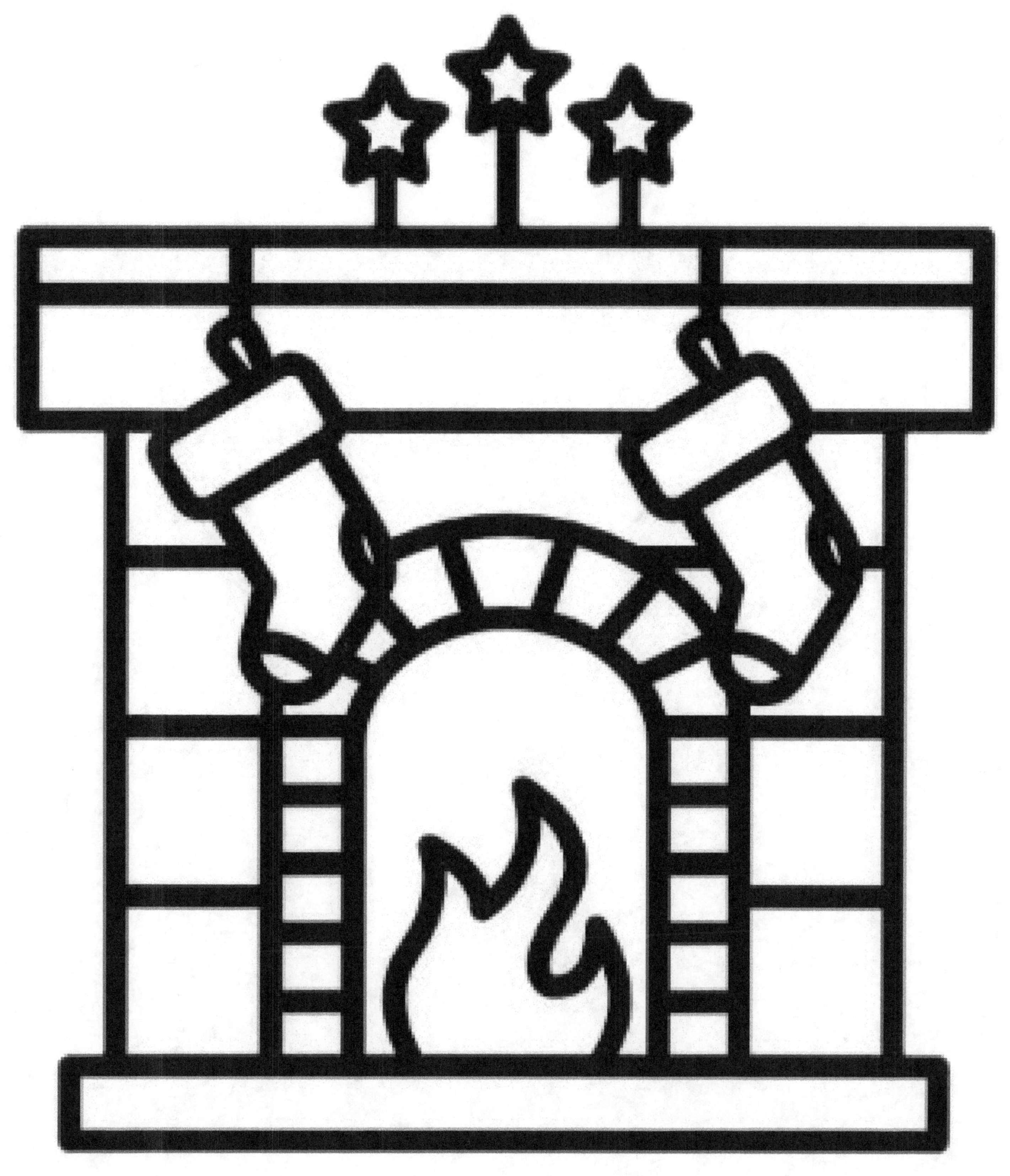

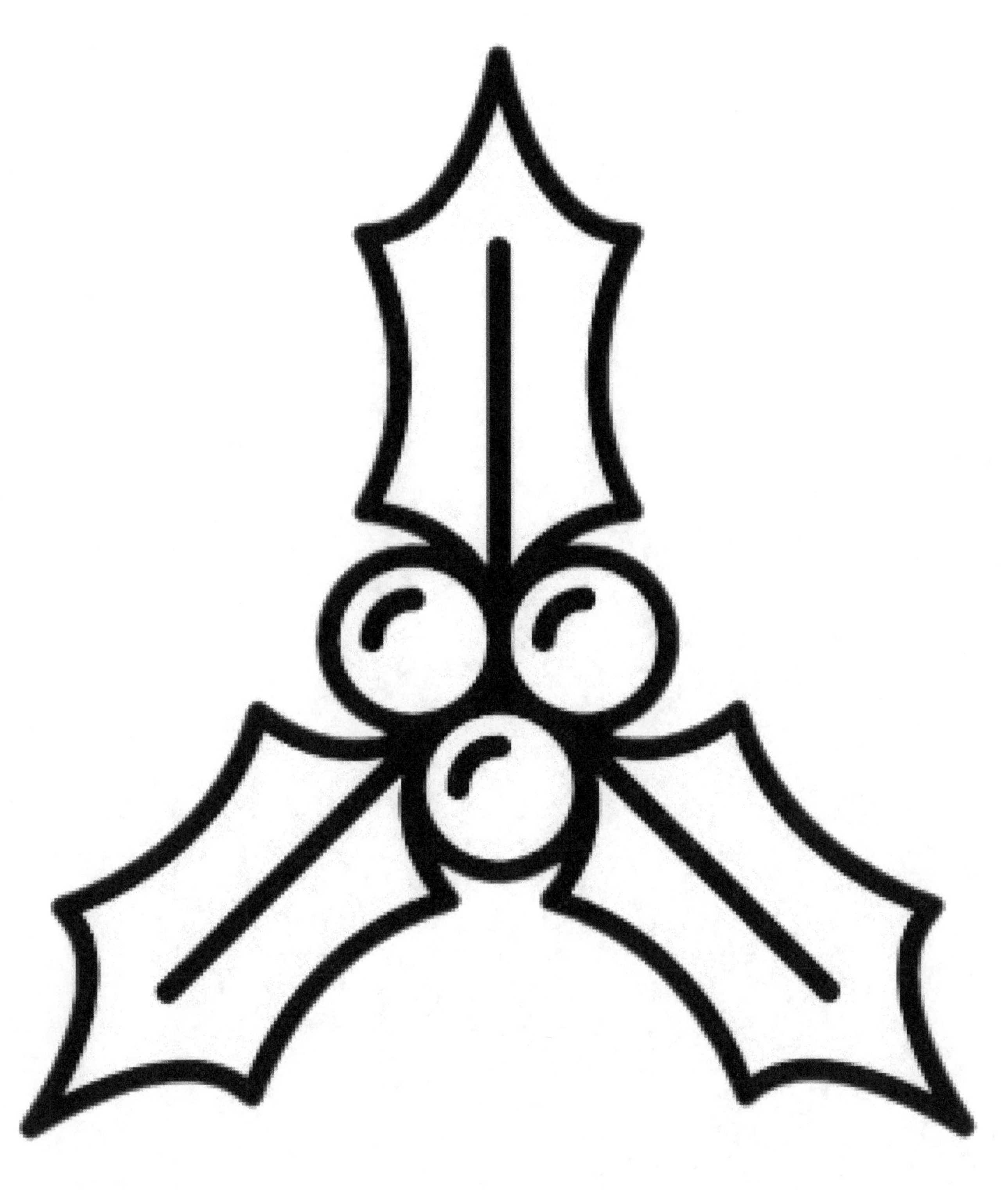

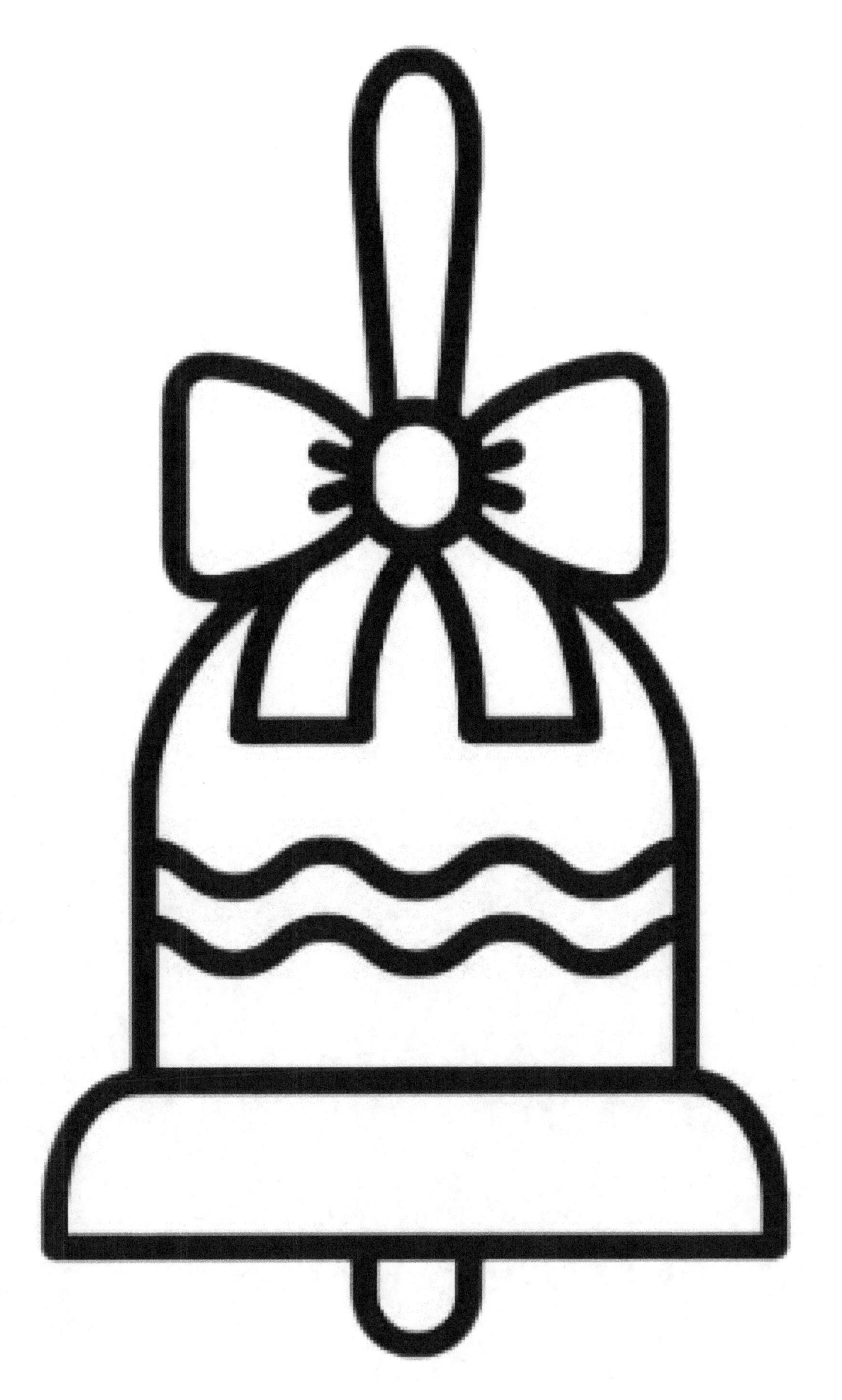

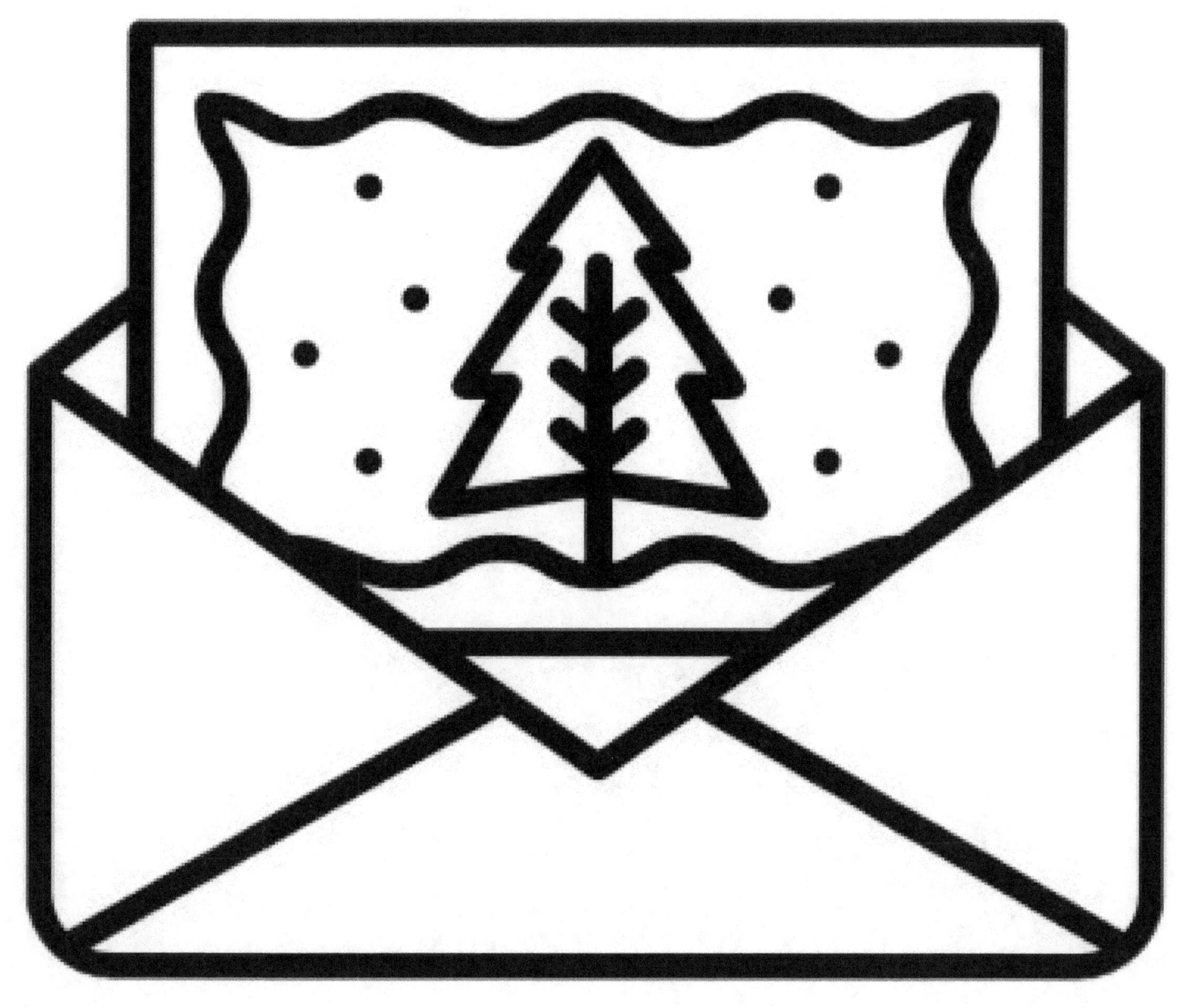

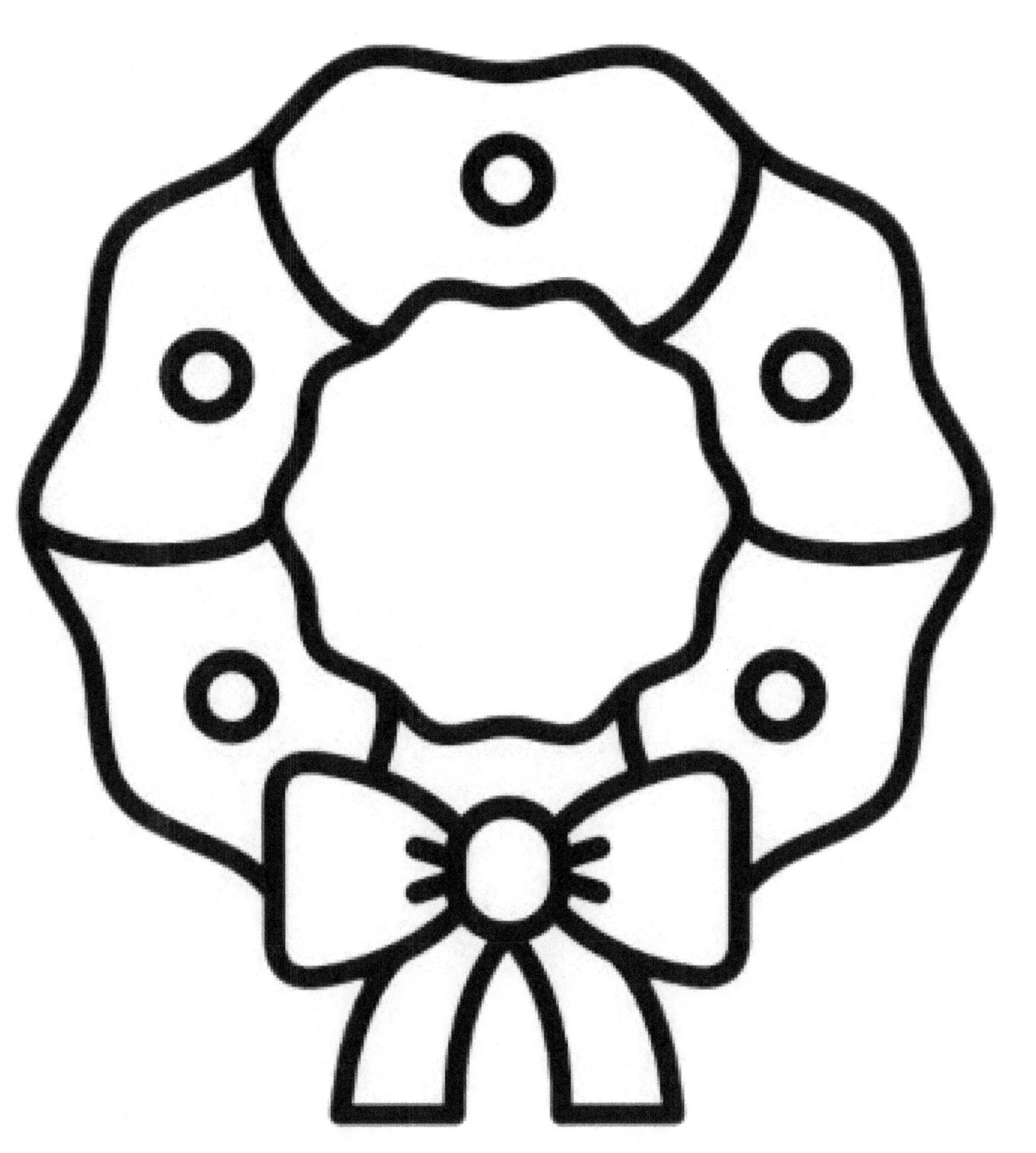

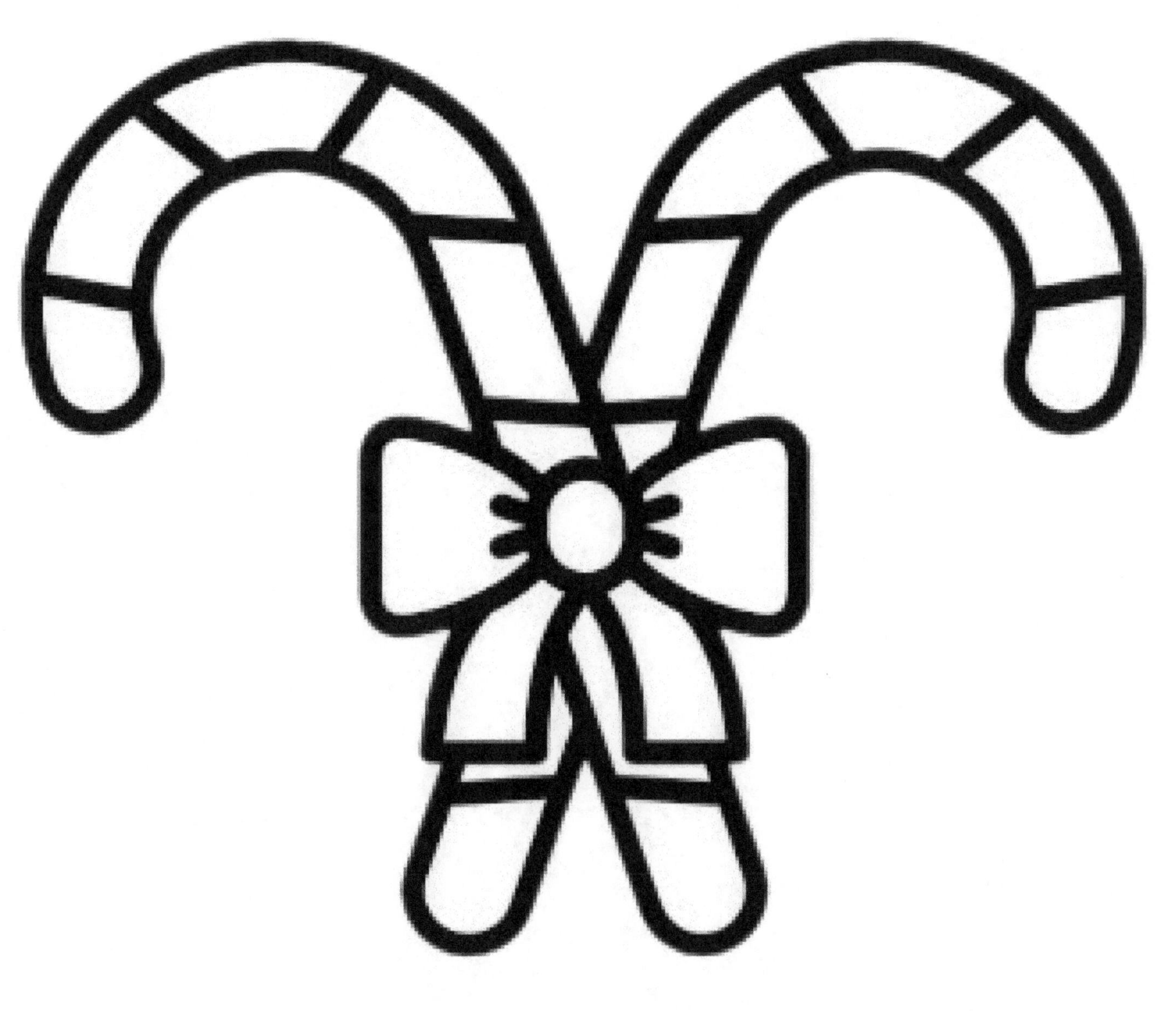

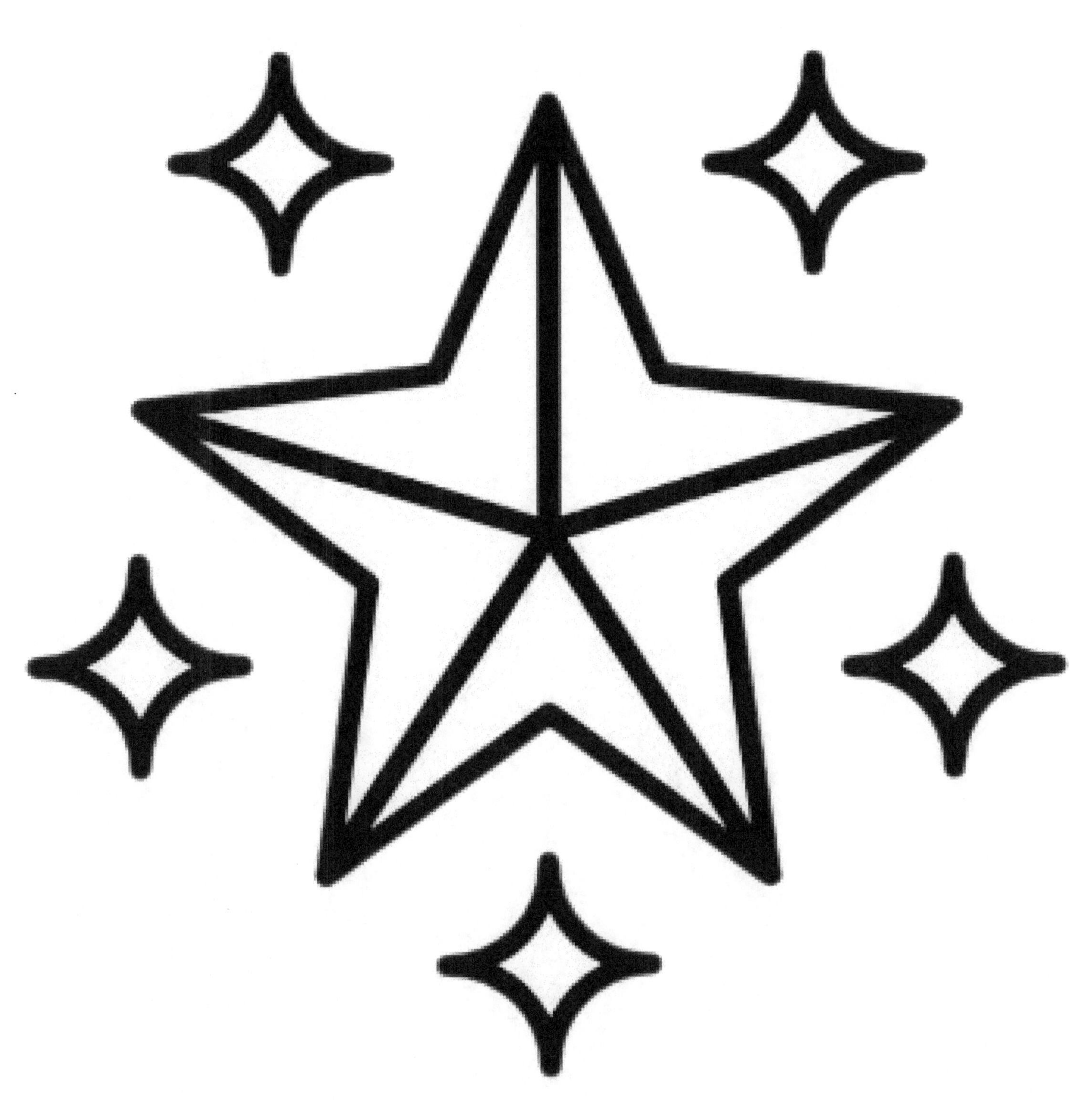

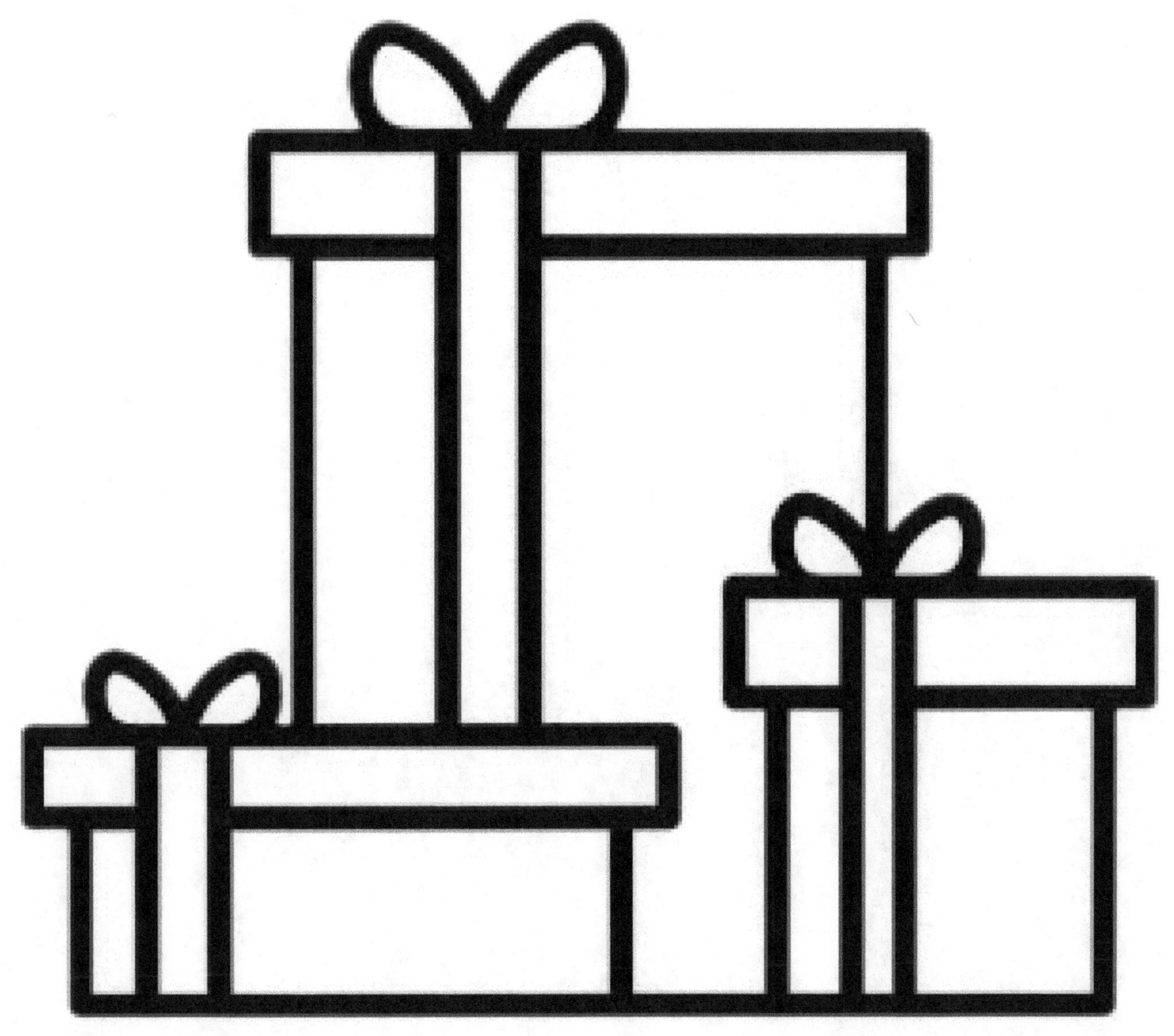

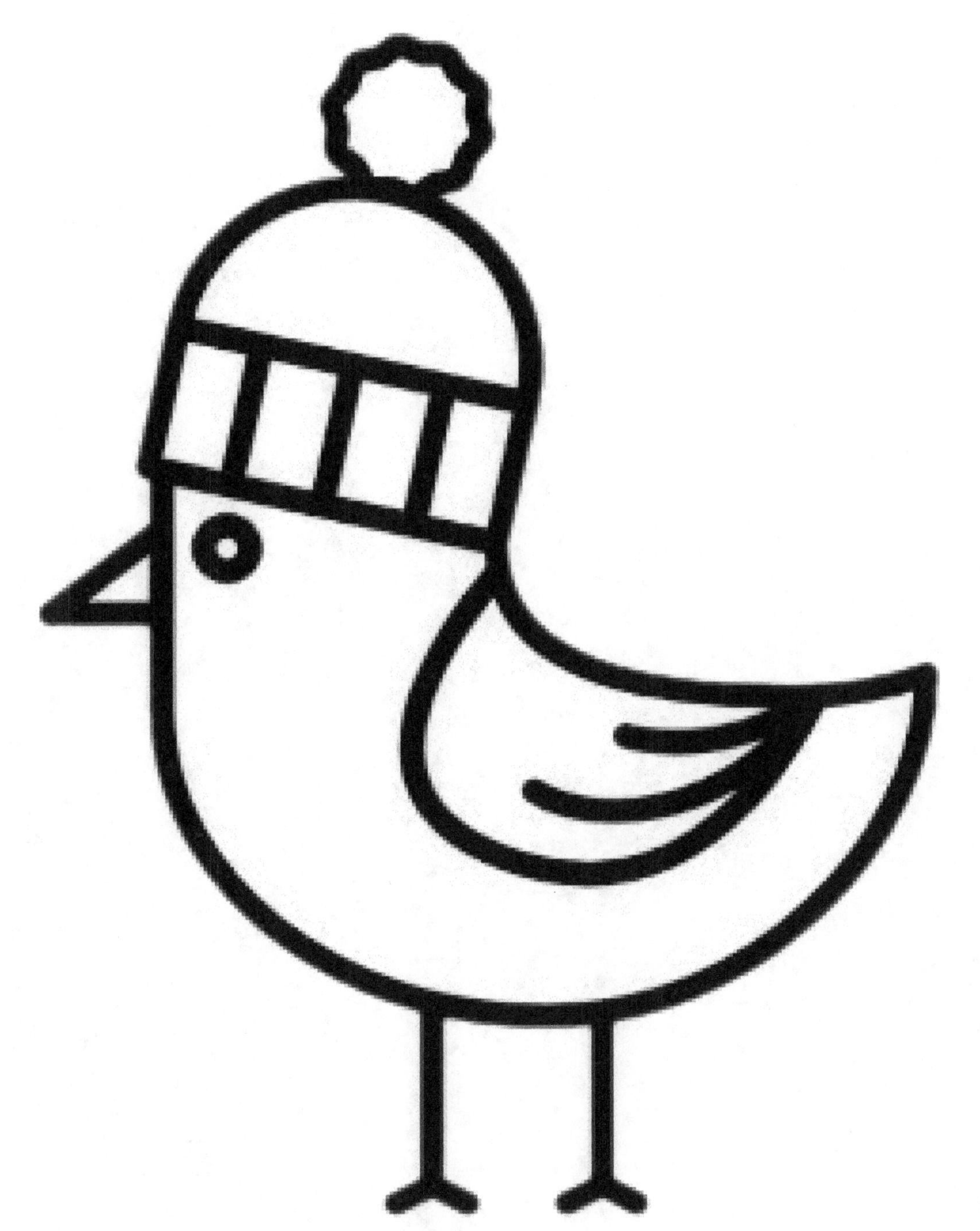

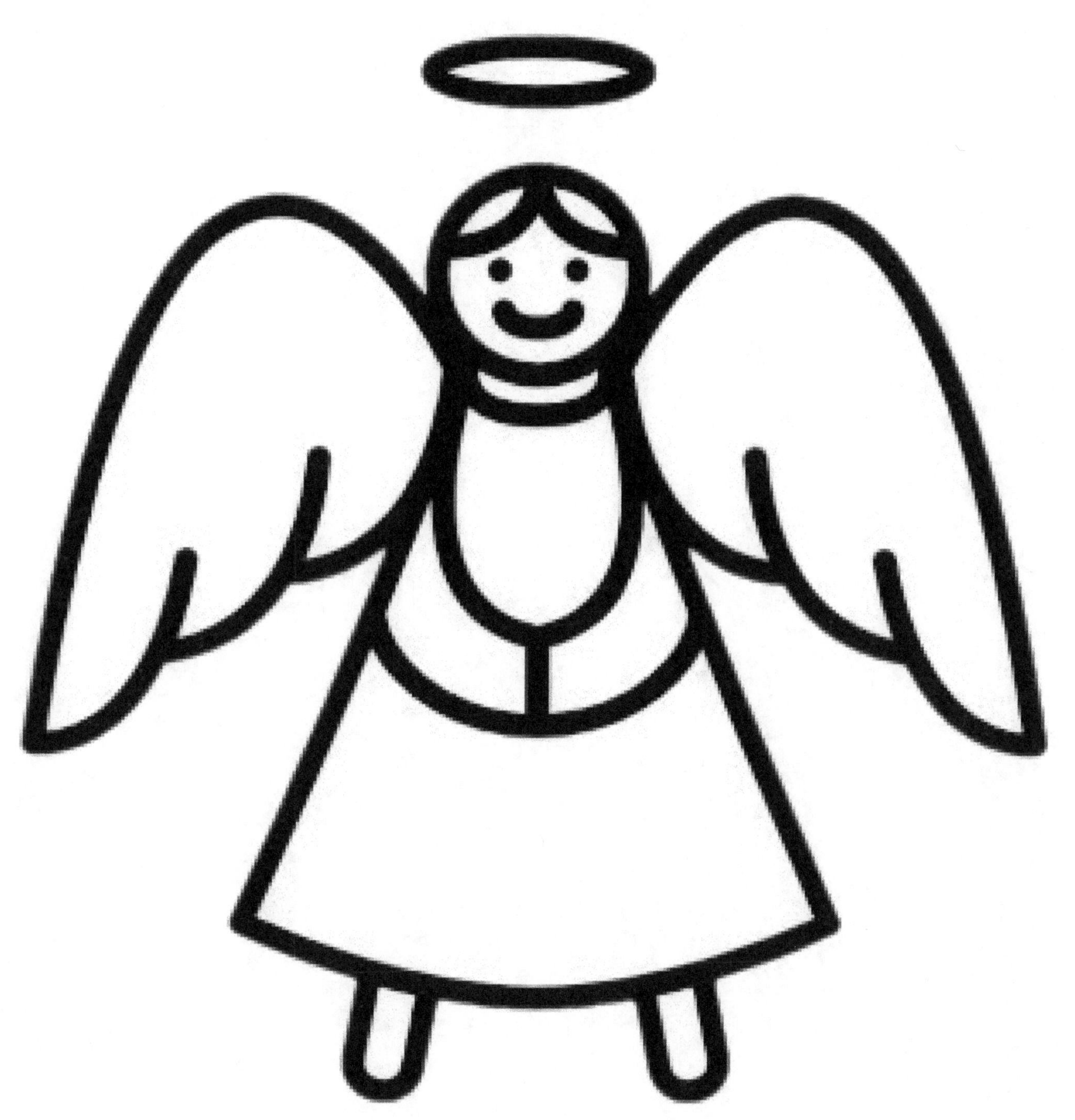

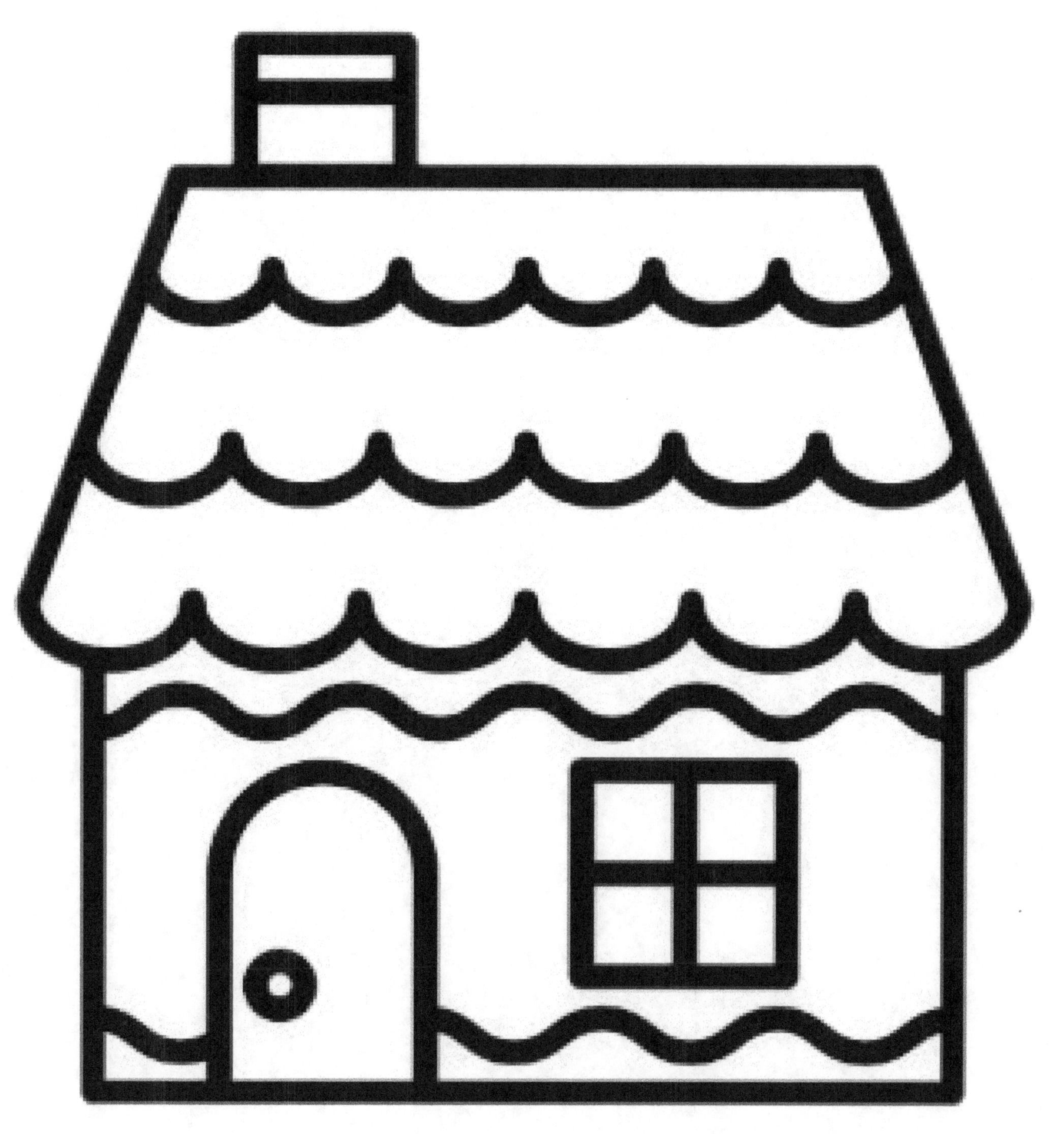

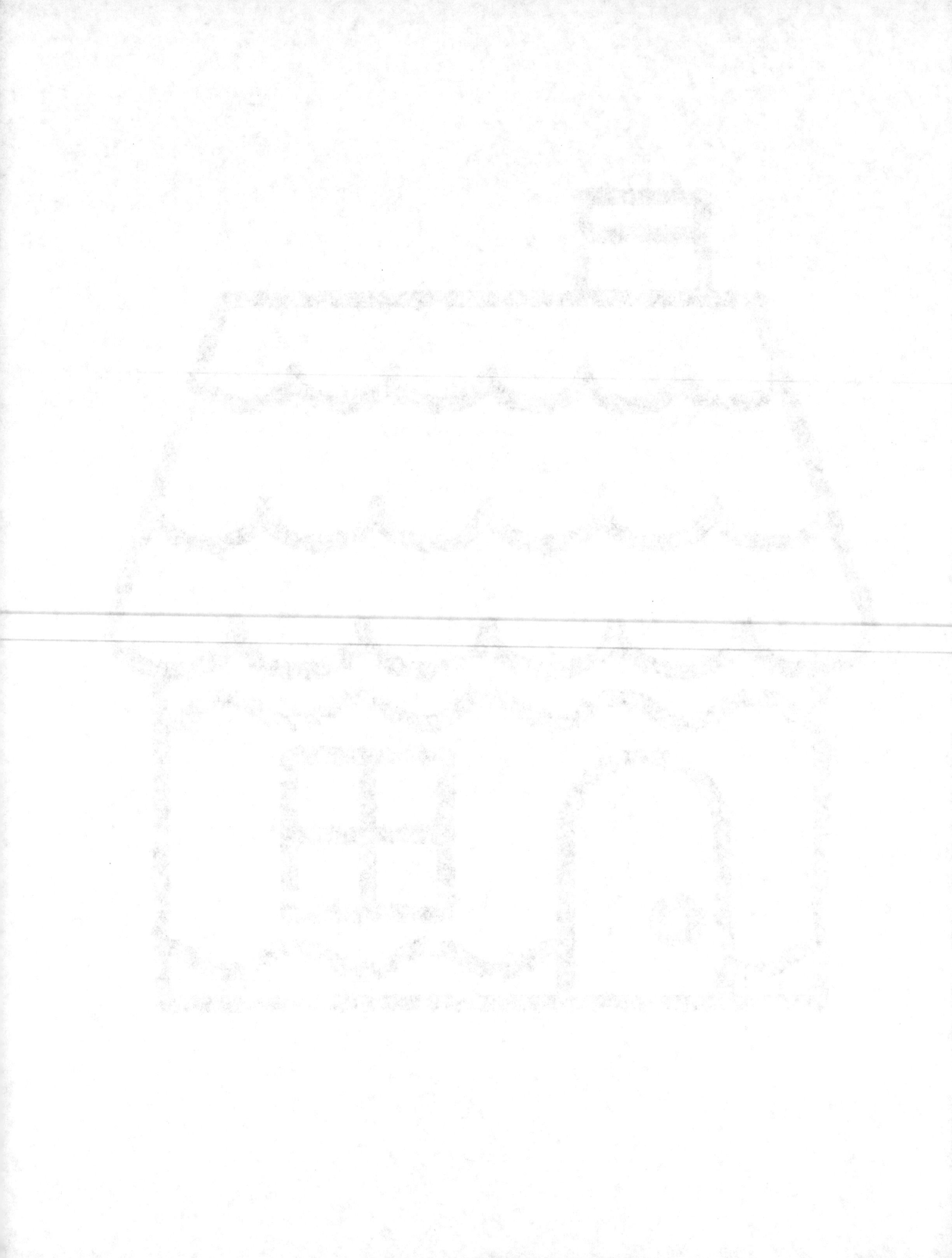

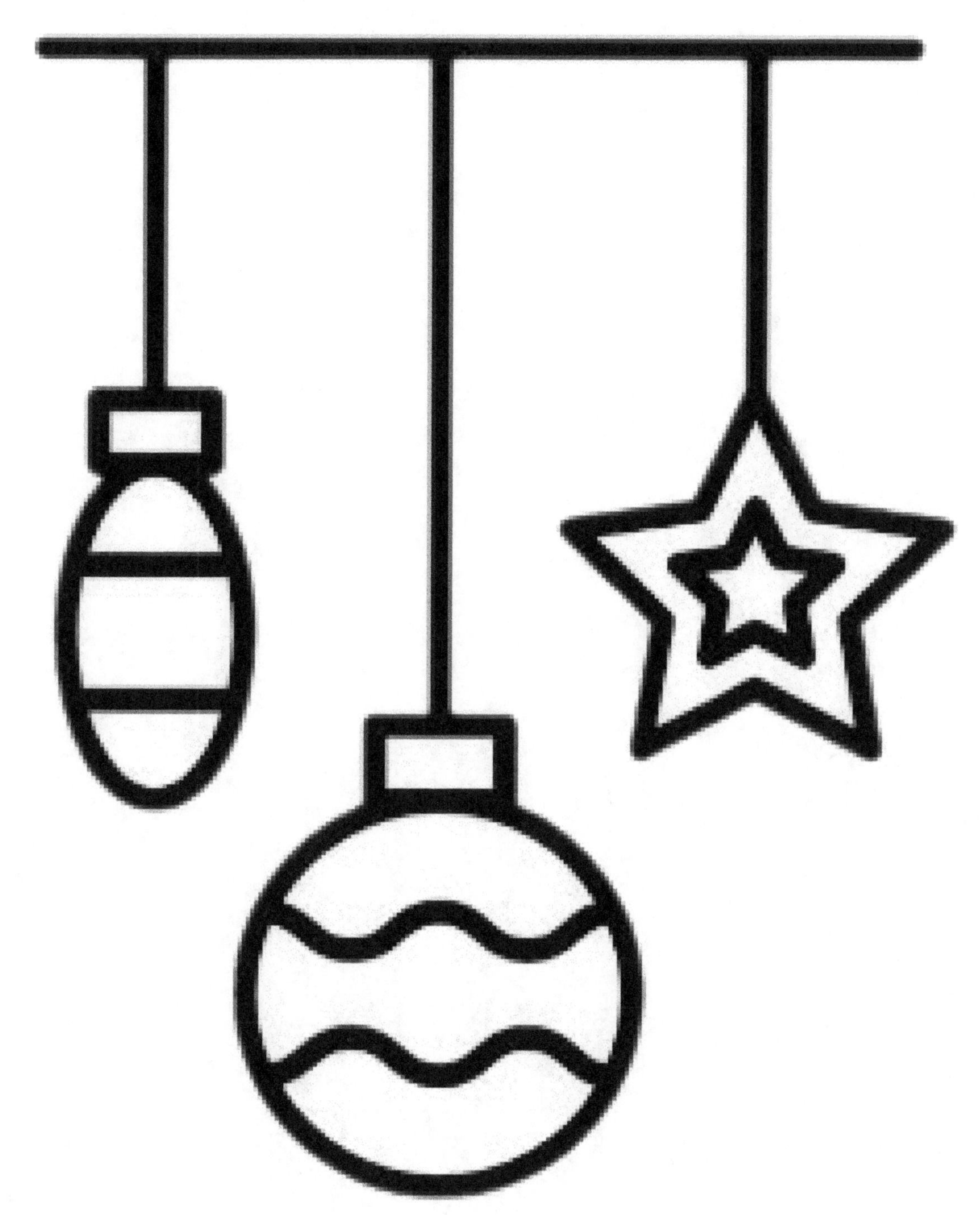

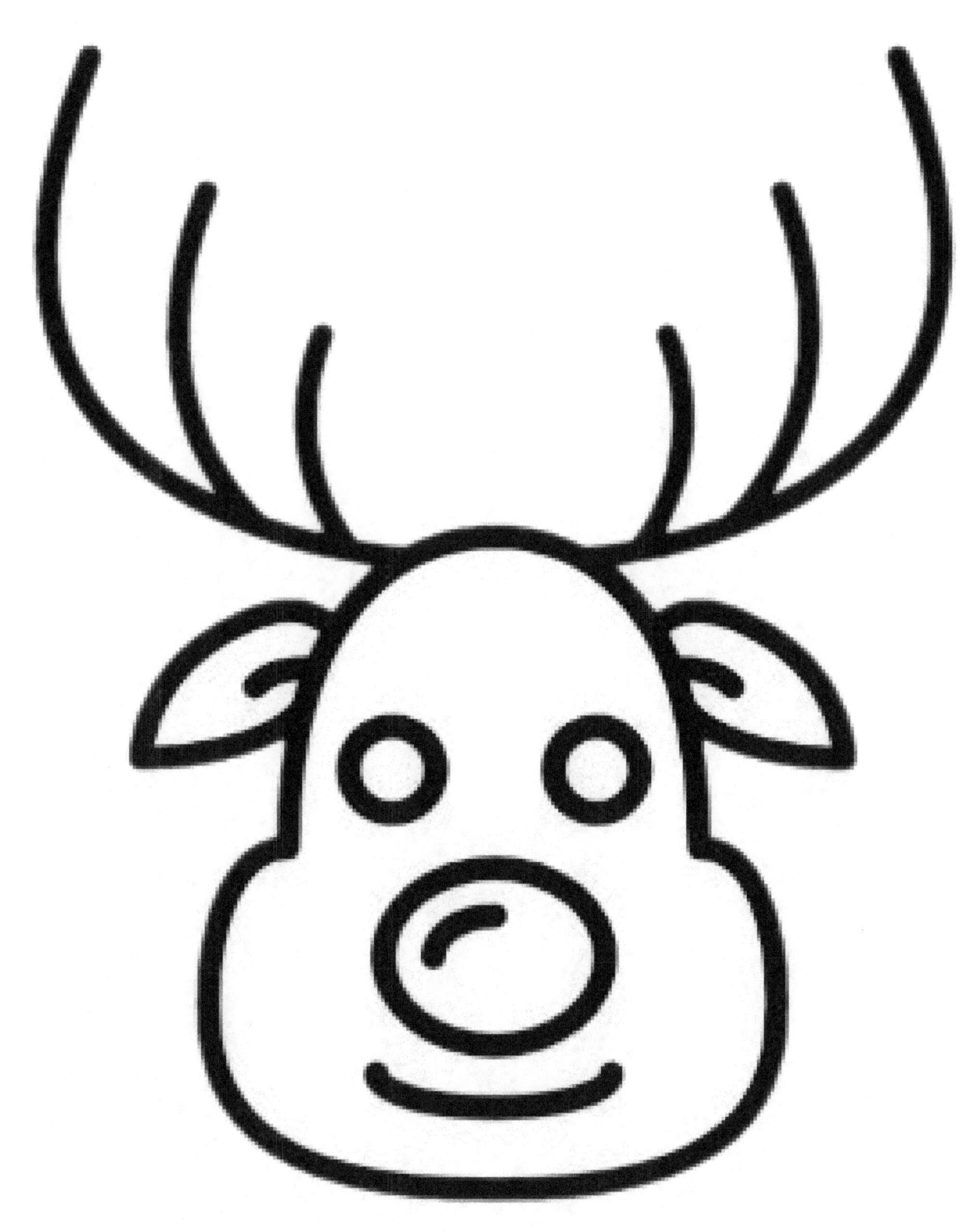

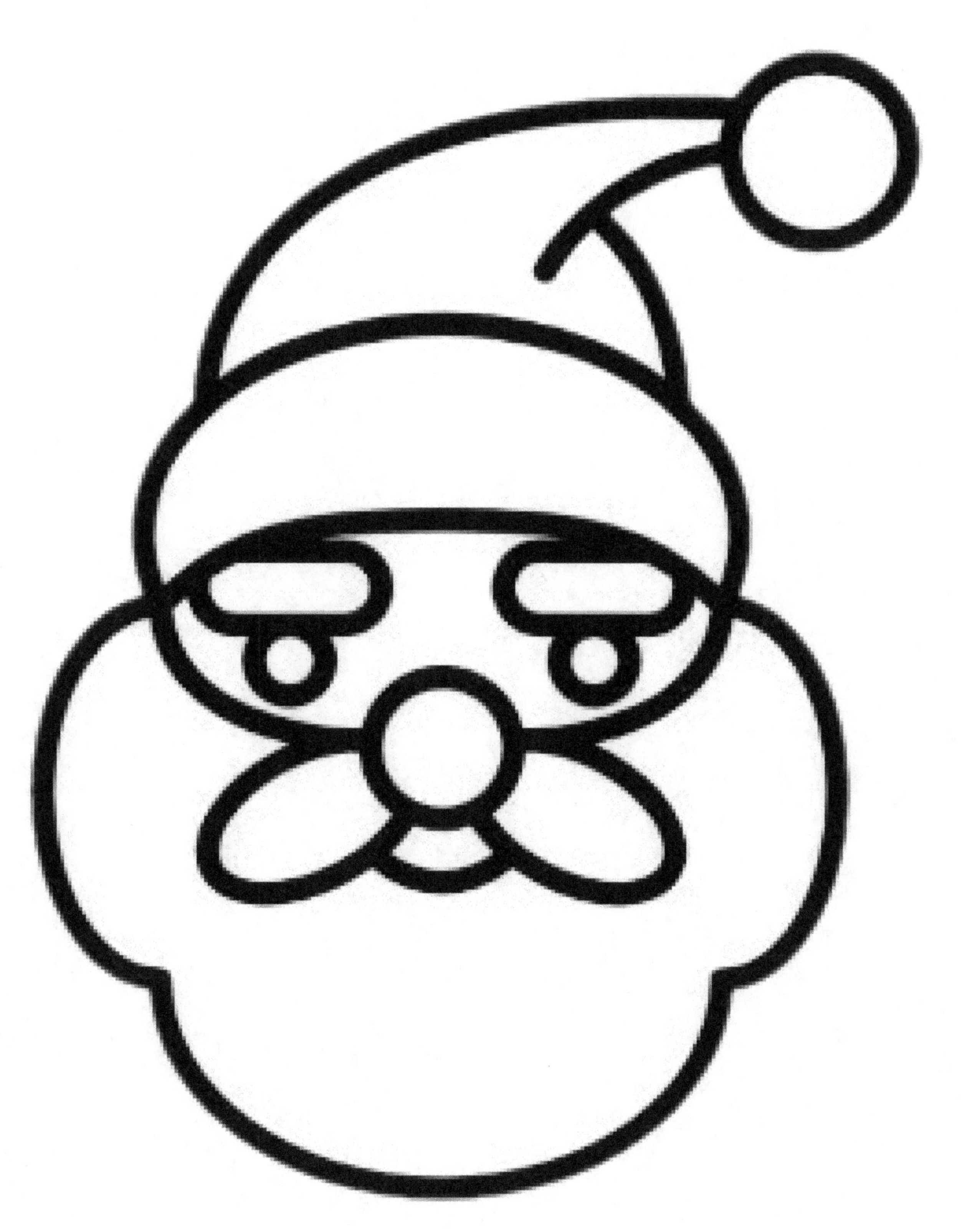

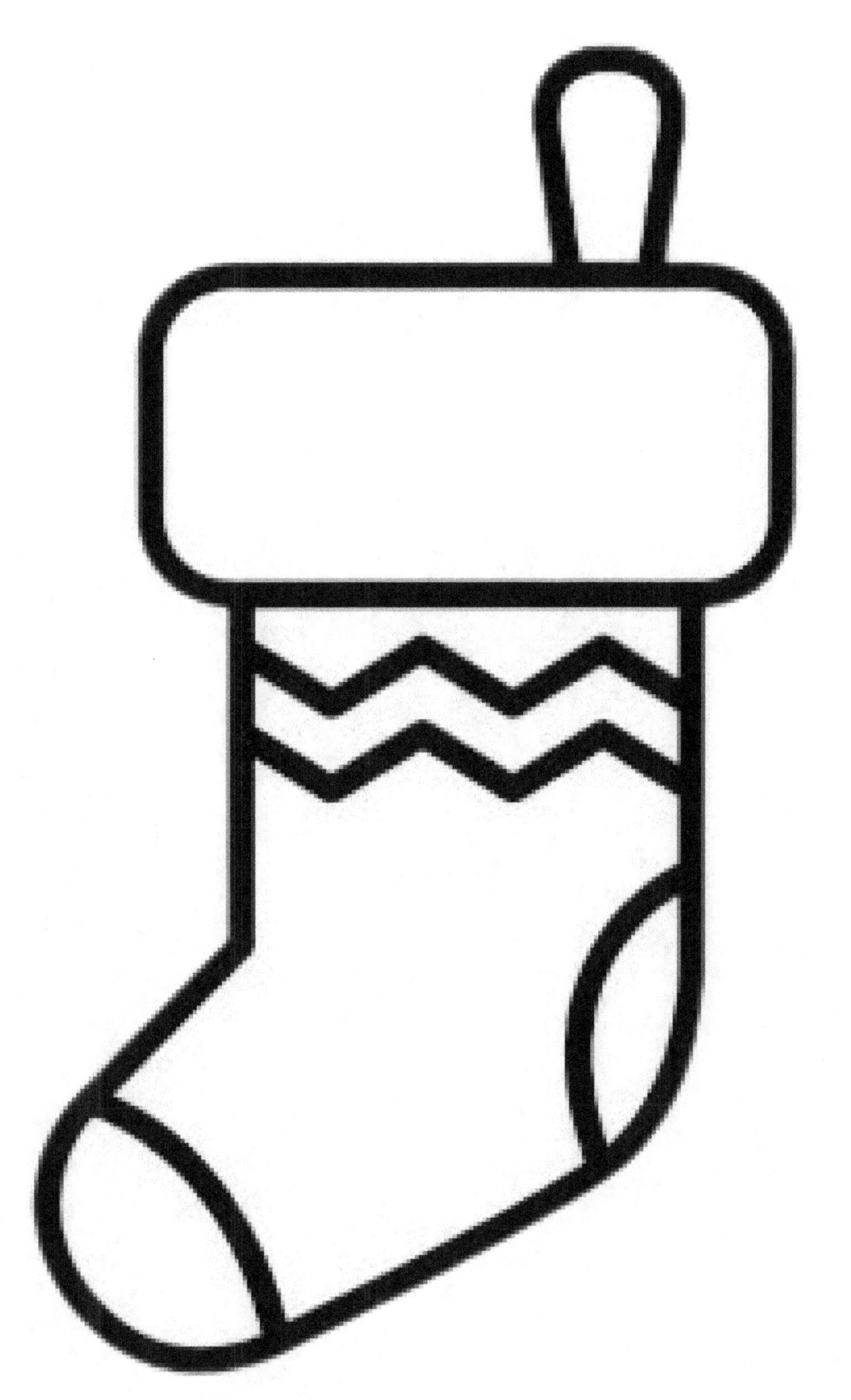

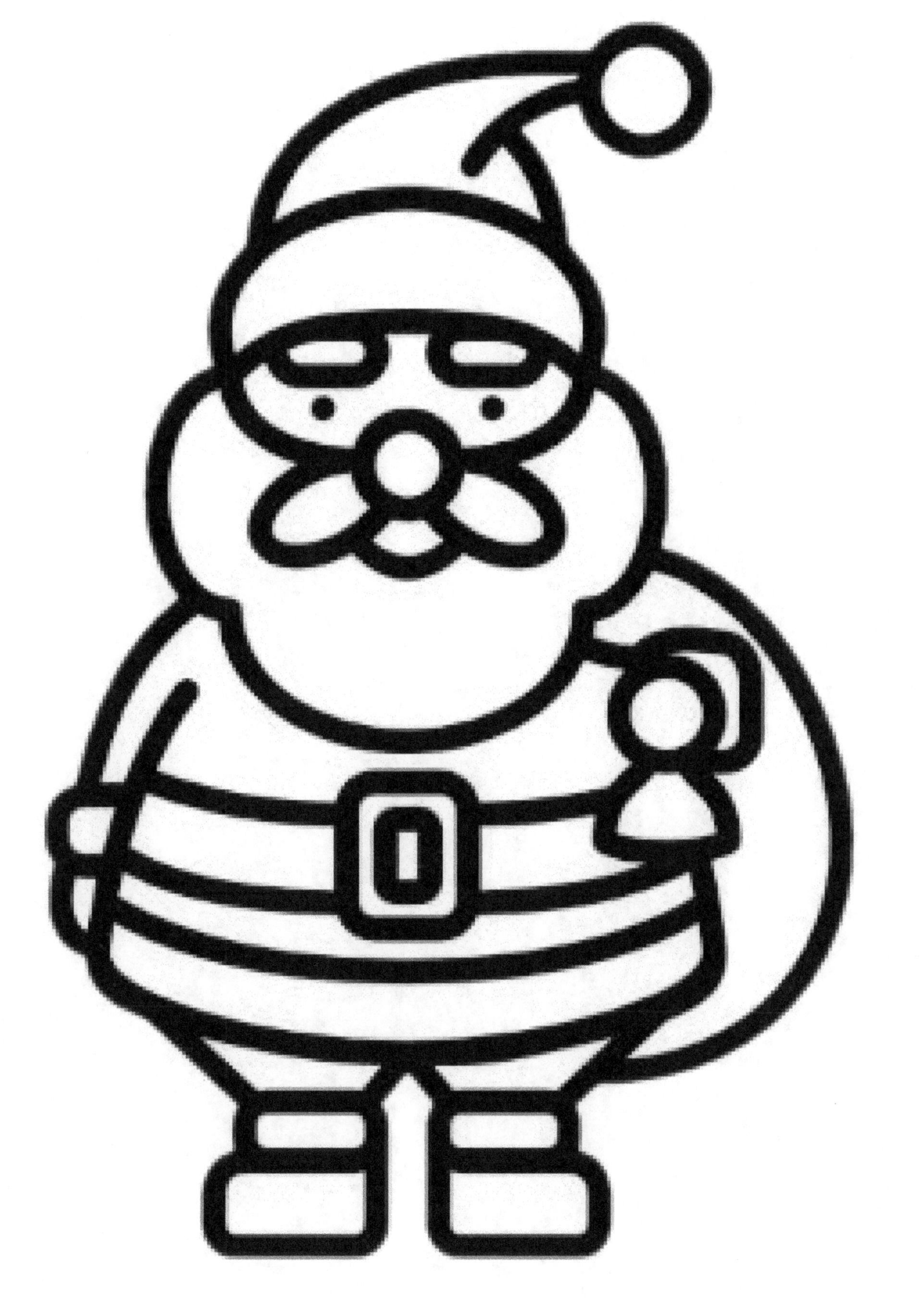